Animals with Super Powers

Glow-in-the-Dark Animals

by Natalie Lunis

Consultant: Edith Widder, Ph.D.
CEO, President & Senior Scientist
Ocean Research & Conservation Association, Inc.

BEARPORT
PUBLISHING

New York, New York

Credits

Cover and Title Page, © Terry Priest/Visuals Unlimited, Inc.; 4L, © Dwight Kuhn/Dwight Kuhn Photography; 4R, © Edith Widder/Ocean Research & Conservation Association, Inc.; 5T, © Kim Taylor/Warren Photographic; 5B, © NaturePL/ SuperStock; 6, © age fotostock/SuperStock; 7T, © Dwight Kuhn/Dwight Kuhn Photography; 7B, © JTB Photo/SuperStock; 8, © Michael & Patricia Fogden/Minden Pictures/NGS Images; 9, © Brian Brake/Photo Researchers, Inc.; 10, © Robert Sisson/NGS Images; 11, © Robert Sisson/NGS Images; 12, © Dr. Morley Read/Shutterstock; 13, © G.I. Bernard/OSF/ Photolibrary; 14, © Visuals Unlimited/Corbis; 15, © Frank LLosa/Frankly.com; 16, Courtesy of Dr. Deheyn, Scripps Institution of Oceanography; 17, Courtesy of Dr. Deheyn, Scripps Institution of Oceanography; 18, © Norbert Wu/Minden Pictures/NGS Images; 19, © NaturePL/SuperStock; 20, © Edith Widder/Ocean Research & Conservation Association, Inc.; 21, © Edith Widder/Ocean Research & Conservation Association, Inc.; 22T, © Dwight Kuhn/Dwight Kuhn Photography; 22B, © Dr. Morley Read/Shutterstock; 23, © Norbert Wu/Minden Pictures/Getty Images.

Publisher: Kenn Goin
Editorial Director: Adam Siegel
Creative Director: Spencer Brinker
Design: Dawn Beard Creative
Cover: Kim Jones
Photo Researcher: Picture Perfect Professionals, LLC

Library of Congress Cataloging-in-Publication Data

Lunis, Natalie.
  Glow-in-the-dark animals / by Natalie Lunis.
    p. cm. — (Animals with super powers)
  Includes bibliographical references and index.
  ISBN-13: 978-1-61772-119-9 (library binding)
  ISBN-10: 1-61772-119-0 (library binding)
  1. Bioluminescence—Juvenile literature. I. Title.
  QH641.L86 2011
  572'.43581—dc22
                        2010038281

For more information, write to Bearport Publishing Company, Inc., 101 Fifth Avenue, Suite 6R, New York, New York 10003. Printed in the United States of America in North Mankato, Minnesota.

121510
10810CGB

10 9 8 7 6 5 4 3 2 1

Contents

Living Lights

Flip a switch and a pitch-black room can suddenly become filled with light. Yet the light that brightens up a dark world doesn't always come from bulbs, wires, and electricity. Sometimes it comes from animals!

On warm summer nights, fireflies twinkle like jewels, some in the air and some on the grass. In a huge dark cave, tiny worm-like creatures **illuminate** the ceiling with a blue glow. Deep down in the sea, a jellyfish sends out flashes of bright blue.

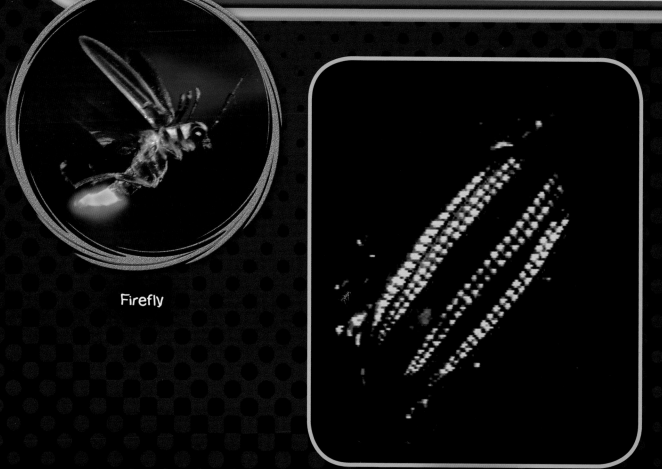

Firefly

Comb jelly

The light from these animals is called **bioluminescence**. *Bio* means "life" or "living," and *luminescence* means "light"—so the source of the brightness is living light. In this book, you will meet eight bioluminescent, or glow-in-the-dark, animals. In some cases, it's clear how their special power helps them survive. In other cases, the light's purpose is still unknown. The animals' glow is as mysterious as it is beautiful.

Cucujo

Anglerfish

Fireflies

Fireflies are the most familiar of all glowing animals. For many people, their twinkling yellow lights are one of the most beautiful—and magical—sights that can be seen on a summer night. Yet the **insects** don't put on their light show for people. As they flash on and off, the fireflies are signaling to others of their own kind.

Males fly through the air as they display their on-and-off light pattern. Females usually rest on the ground or on a blade of grass as they signal back. The fireflies are trying to find each other in order to **mate**. The eggs that the female lays after mating will grow into a new set of twinkling night lights.

There are more than 2,000 **species**, or kinds, of fireflies. Each species has a different timing for flashing its light on and off.

Fireflies are not really flies. Instead, they belong to a large group of insects known as beetles.

The part of a firefly that lights up is its abdomen, which is the rear section of its body.

In Florida and other warm places, fireflies can be spotted during many months of the year.

New Zealand Glowworm

Glowworms aren't really worms—though they do glow. The wiggly little creatures are actually the **larvae**, or young form, of different kinds of insects.

Surprisingly, the world's most famous glowworms live in a hidden, hard-to-reach place. Their home is the Waitomo (wye-TOH-moh) Caves in New Zealand. There, in an area known as the Glowworm **Grotto**, hundreds of thousands of the little larvae cling to the ceiling. Each one is in a clear tube-shaped nest with sticky threads hanging down. Together, the tiny glowworms— each about one inch (2.5 cm) long—give off enough light to cast a bright blue glow on the cave's ceiling.

glowworm

The New Zealand glowworm makes its sticky threads to catch food. Small flying insects, attracted to the glowworm's light, fly into the threads and get stuck. Then the glowworm pulls up the threads and eats the insects.

New Zealand glowworms grow to become little flies—which do not glow. The female flies lay sticky eggs on the ceiling of the cave, and new glowworms hatch from the eggs.

A small river runs through the Waitomo Caves. As a result, visitors can view the caves—and the glowworms above their heads—from boats.

Railroad Worm

Most bioluminescent animals glow only in one color. A few kinds, however, have multicolored lights. One of them is the **larva**, or young form, of a beetle that lives in South America. This worm-like creature has a glowing red head and yellow lights along its body. People call it the railroad worm because it looks like a train traveling through the night—with a red light in front and brightly lit windows in the cars behind.

What causes a railroad worm's red and yellow glow? Inside the insect's body, special **chemicals** mix with **oxygen** to turn on these train lights. Even though fireflies and New Zealand glowworms do not give off the same colors, their glow comes from these substances, too.

Male railroad worm

Female railroad worm

Female railroad worms grow to be up to two inches (5 cm) long. Males are much smaller.

Railroad worms mostly stay hidden away under rocks and fallen leaves. Their bodies light up only when they are touched or disturbed. Scientists think that the flash of light might be a way of startling enemies and scaring them away.

Cucujo

The cucujo (koo-KOO-joh) is a South American beetle that gives off plenty of light as an adult. In fact, these insects glow so brightly that people have used them as lamps.

A cucujo's bright light comes mainly from two spots that look like headlights at the front of its body. The insect also has an area that lights up on its underside, but this light can be seen only when the cucujo is flying.

For a long time, **native people** in parts of South America collected cucujos for their light. Sometimes they kept the glowing insects in cages, which then became working lanterns. Sometimes they put the cucujos into **gauze** bags. They then tied the bags to their heads or feet to light their way as they walked through a dark forest.

The cucujo is very large for an insect. An adult can be two inches (5 cm) long.

The cucujo is the brightest of all bioluminescent insects. Unlike fireflies, cucujos do not flash. Instead, they glow with a steady light.

The light that cucujos and other bioluminescent animals produce is known as cool light. It gives off very little heat—unlike electric light, which gives off a great deal of heat.

Dinoflagellates

Thousands of different species of bioluminescent animals live on land, but far more live in the sea. In fact, scientists think that most sea creatures that live in the **open ocean** make light in one way or another.

Dinoflagellates (dye-nuh-FLAJ-uh-*lets*) are one of the sea's tiniest glow-in-the-dark animals. Each one is so small that a person needs a **microscope** to see it. Dinoflagellates swim at the ocean's surface. Sometimes millions of these creatures float together in a mass. They do not glow, however, unless something such as a boat passes through them and disturbs them. Then the dinoflagellates all light up at once, covering the water with shimmering swirls.

This dinoflagellate, photographed under a powerful microscope, is shown many times larger than its actual size.

Sometimes the action of a wave, the wind, or swimming fish causes dinoflagellates to light up.

When they light up, dinoflagellates give off a bluish-green flash.

Fireworms

Like fireflies, fireworms that glow use light to signal for mates—but they do so in the water, not on land. To attract males, females swim near the surface of the sea and **spew** glowing green **mucus** into the water. Along with the mucus, they release tiny eggs. Males see the glow and swim toward it. They **fertilize** the eggs so that new fireworms can hatch.

After hatching, young fireworms spew out their own mucus and produce flashing green light. Since they are too young to **reproduce**, they do not put on this light show to attract mates. Scientists think that, instead, the green light confuses fish and other hungry animals that might try to eat the little sea worms.

The kind of fireworm that gives off a green glow is one to four inches (2.5 to 10 cm) long and lives in warm, shallow ocean waters.

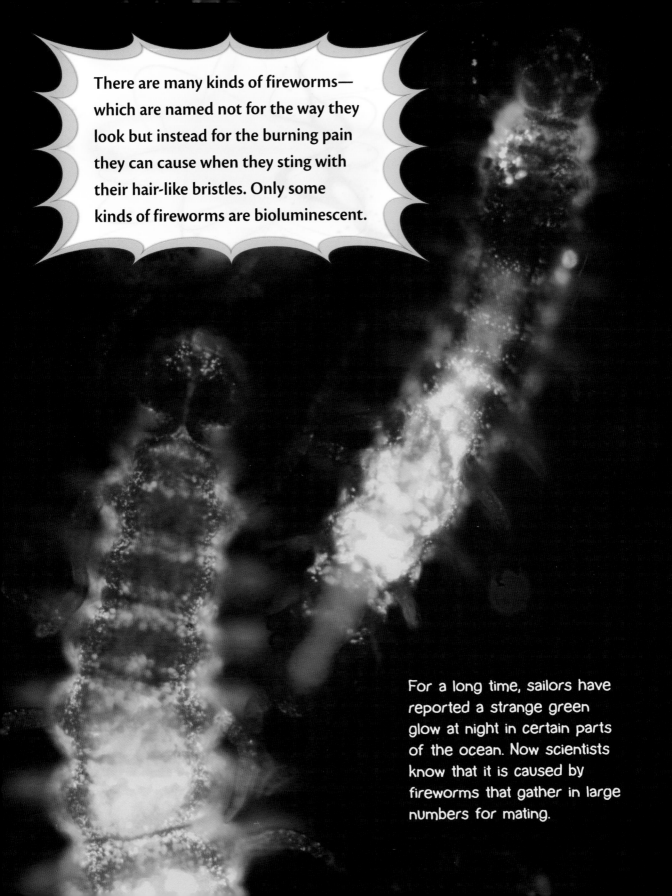

There are many kinds of fireworms—which are named not for the way they look but instead for the burning pain they can cause when they sting with their hair-like bristles. Only some kinds of fireworms are bioluminescent.

For a long time, sailors have reported a strange green glow at night in certain parts of the ocean. Now scientists know that it is caused by fireworms that gather in large numbers for mating.

Anglerfish

"Angler" is an old-fashioned word for someone who fishes with a rod and a line. The person fishing usually places a piece of live **bait**, such as a worm, or other kind of **lure** at the end. An anglerfish also fishes with a rod and lure, but they are part of its own body. Because the anglerfish lives in the deep sea, a place that almost no sunlight reaches, the lure it uses has a bioluminescent glow.

Other deep-sea fish are attracted to the anglerfish's worm-like bait. Thinking it is about to catch something good to eat, one of these fish swims over to grab its next meal. Instead, however, it becomes a meal for the anglerfish, which quickly snaps the creature up into its mouth.

This anglerfish is

The light given off by the anglerfish's "bait" is not made by the fish itself. Instead, the glow comes from bioluminescent **bacteria**, tiny living things that make their home—and light—inside the tip of the anglerfish's fishing rod.

bioluminescent lure

The anglerfish's big, sharp teeth help it grab its victim.

Deep-sea Jellyfish

The deep sea is a dark and dangerous place. To increase their chances of survival, some bioluminescent animals use light as an alarm system. One of these creatures is the deep-sea jellyfish. When it is about to be eaten by an enemy, it turns its flashing lights up all the way. Hopefully, the lights will attract an even bigger and scarier creature—which might then attack the attacker.

This behavior, which scientists call the "burglar alarm display," is one of many surprising discoveries about bioluminescent animals. However, there is much more work to be done. For example, many of the animal species on Earth have not yet been discovered. What other glowing creatures exist? How does their special ability help them survive? Can discoveries about glow-in-the-dark animals help people? Scientists are working to shed light on these questions.

There are many kinds of bioluminescent jellyfish. This one, the comb jelly, produces bright blue flashes to startle its enemies.

Deep-sea jellyfish, such as this one flashing a "burglar alarm," aren't really fish. That's why some people call them "sea jellies."

Some scientists are investigating whether bioluminescence might lead to new medical treatments, including ones for cancer.

More About Glow-in-the-Dark Animals

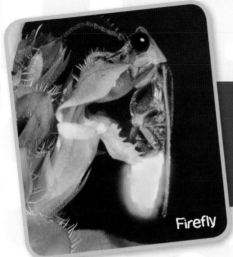
Firefly

○ Fireflies are also known as "lightning bugs."

○ Frogs and toads like to eat fireflies. Sometimes, after they have eaten many of the glowing insects, their stomachs—which are covered by thin, light-colored skin—also give off a glow.

○ In Japan, firefly festivals are held in different places each year to honor the bioluminescent insects. People from all over the country and around the world visit to see real fireflies, as well as pictures of the insects made by children and people who are dressed in firefly costumes.

◉ In parts of South America, women have put cucujos in gauze bags and worn them as decorations in their hair.

Cucujo

○ When under attack, deep-sea squids can squirt out a cloud of bioluminescent ink. The glowing cloud attracts the attention of the squid's enemy. In the meantime, the squid quickly gets away.

Glossary

bacteria (bak-TEER-ee-uh) tiny life forms that can be seen only under a microscope

bait (BAYT) food used to attract an animal to a trap

bioluminescence (*bye*-oh-loo-muh-NES-unhss) light made by living things

chemicals (KEM-uh-kuhlz) natural or human-made substances

fertilize (FUR-tuh-lize) to make an egg able to produce young

gauze (GAWZ) a very thin fabric that one can see through

grotto (GROT-oh) a cave

illuminate (i-LOO-muh-nayt) to light

insects (IN-sekts) small animals that have six legs, three main body parts, two antennas, and a hard covering called an exoskeleton

larva (LAR-vuh) a young insect that has a worm-like body; singular form of *larvae*

larvae (LAR-vee) young insects that have worm-like bodies; plural form of *larva*

lure (LOOR) something that attracts an animal, often leading it into a trap

mate (MAYT) to come together to have young

microscope (MYE-kruh-skohp) a tool that scientists use to see things that are too small to see with the eyes alone

mucus (MYOO-kuhss) a sticky liquid made by an animal

native people (NAY-tiv PEE-puhl) people belonging to a particular place because of where they were born

open ocean (OH-puhn OH-shuhn) ocean waters that are away from land and away from the ocean floor

oxygen (OK-suh-juhn) a colorless gas that is found in the air and water, and that animals and people need to breathe

reproduce (*ree*-pruh-DOOSS) to have young

species (SPEE-sheez) groups that animals are divided into, according to similar characteristics; members of the same species can have offspring together

spew (SPYOO) to send out of the mouth or body; to spit

Index

Bibliography

Science Daily. "Decoding Mysterious Green Glow of the Sea." (www.sciencedaily.com/releases/2009/04/090401134606.htm)

Simon, Hilda. *Living Lanterns: Luminescence in Animals*. New York: Viking (1971).

Widder, Edie. "Glowing in the Dark." *Nova Science Now.* (www.pbs.org/wgbh/nova/sciencenow/0305/04-glow-01.html)

Read More

Collard, Sneed B., III. *In the Deep Sea*. Tarrytown, NY: Marshall Cavendish (2006).

Hirschmann, Kris. *Glow-in-the-Dark Animals*. New York: Scholastic (2004).

Widder, Edith. *The Bioluminescence Coloring Book*. Fort Pierce, FL: Harbor Branch Oceanographic Institution (2003).

Learn More Online

To learn more about glow-in-the-dark animals, visit
www.bearportpublishing.com/AnimalswithSuperPowers

About the Author

Natalie Lunis has written many science and nature books for children. She watches for fireflies in the Hudson River Valley, just north of New York City.